Welcom

Guest Name: _____ Date Stayed: _____

Traveling From: _____ Weather: ☀ ⛅ ☂ ❄ 🌡 🌡 🚩 ☁

Favorite Memory / Recommended Activity:

_____

_____

_____

_____

Message:

_____

_____

_____

_____

_____

_____

May we share your message?   Yes / No

Guest Name: _____ Date Stayed: _____

Traveling From: _____ Weather: ☀ ⛅ ☂ ❄ 🌡 🌡 🚩 ☁

Favorite Memory / Recommended Activity:

_____

_____

_____

_____

_____

Message:

_____

_____

_____

_____

_____

_____

_____

May we share your message?   Yes / No

Guest Name: _____ Date Stayed: _____

Traveling From: _____ Weather: ☀ ⛅ ☔ ❄ 🌡 🌡 🚩 ☁

Favorite Memory / Recommended Activity:

_____

_____

_____

_____

Message:

_____

_____

_____

_____

_____

_____

May we share your message?   Yes / No

Guest Name: _____   Date Stayed: _____

Traveling From: _____   Weather: ☀ ☁ ☂ ❄ 🌡 🌡 🚩 ☁

Favorite Memory / Recommended Activity:

_____

_____

_____

_____

Message:

_____

_____

_____

_____

_____

_____

May we share your message?   Yes / No

Guest Name: _____ Date Stayed: _____

Traveling From: _____ Weather: ☀ ⛅ ☂ ❄ 🌡 🌡 🚩 ☁

Favorite Memory / Recommended Activity:

_____

_____

_____

_____

Message:

_____

_____

_____

_____

_____

_____

May we share your message?   Yes / No

Guest Name: _____ Date Stayed: _____

Traveling From: _____ Weather: ☀ ⛅ ☔ ❄ 🌡 🌡 🚩 ☁

Favorite Memory / Recommended Activity:

_____

_____

_____

_____

Message:

_____

_____

_____

_____

_____

_____

May we share your message?   Yes / No

Guest Name: _____   Date Stayed: _____

Traveling From: _____   Weather: ☀ ⛅ ☔ ❄ 🌡 🌡 🚩 ☁

Favorite Memory / Recommended Activity:

_____

_____

_____

_____

_____

Message:

_____

_____

_____

_____

_____

May we share your message?   Yes / No

Guest Name: _____   Date Stayed: _____

Traveling From: _____   Weather: ☀ ⛅ ☂ ❄ 🌡 🌡 🚩 ☁

Favorite Memory / Recommended Activity:

_____

_____

_____

_____

Message:

_____

_____

_____

_____

_____

_____

May we share your message?   Yes / No

Guest Name: _____ Date Stayed: _____

Traveling From: _____ Weather: ☀ ☁ ☂ ❄ 🌡 🌡 🚩 ☁

Favorite Memory / Recommended Activity:

_____

_____

_____

_____

Message:

_____

_____

_____

_____

_____

_____

May we share your message?   Yes / No

Guest Name: _____ Date Stayed: _____

Traveling From: _____ Weather: ☀ ☁ ☔ ❄ 🌡 🌡 🚩 ☁

Favorite Memory / Recommended Activity:

_____

_____

_____

_____

_____

Message:

_____

_____

_____

_____

_____

_____

May we share your message?   Yes / No

Guest Name: _____ Date Stayed: _____

Traveling From: _____ Weather: ☀ ⛅ ☂ ❄ 🌡 🌡 🚩 ☁

Favorite Memory / Recommended Activity:

_____

_____

_____

_____

_____

Message:

_____

_____

_____

_____

_____

_____

_____

May we share your message?   Yes / No

Guest Name: _____   Date Stayed: _____

Traveling From: _____   Weather: ☀ ☁ ☔ ❄ 🌡 🌡 🏳 ☁

Favorite Memory / Recommended Activity:

_____

_____

_____

_____

Message:

_____

_____

_____

_____

_____

_____

_____

May we share your message?   Yes / No

Guest Name: _____ Date Stayed: _____

Traveling From: _____ Weather: ☀ ⛅ ☔ ❄ 🌡 🌡 🚩 ☁

Favorite Memory / Recommended Activity:

_____

_____

_____

_____

Message:

_____

_____

_____

_____

_____

_____

May we share your message?   Yes / No

Guest Name: _____   Date Stayed: _____

Traveling From: _____   Weather: ☼ ⛅ ☔ ❄ 🌡 🌡 🚩 ☁

Favorite Memory / Recommended Activity:

_____

_____

_____

_____

Message:

_____

_____

_____

_____

_____

_____

_____

May we share your message?   Yes / No

Guest Name: _____ Date Stayed: _____

Traveling From: _____ Weather: ☀ ⛅ ☔ ❄ 🌡 🌡 🚩 ☁

Favorite Memory / Recommended Activity:

_____

_____

_____

_____

Message:

_____

_____

_____

_____

_____

May we share your message?   Yes / No

Guest Name: _____ Date Stayed: _____

Traveling From: _____ Weather: ☀ ☁ ☂ ❄ 🌡 🌡 🚩 ☁

Favorite Memory / Recommended Activity:

_____

_____

_____

_____

_____

Message:

_____

_____

_____

_____

_____

_____

May we share your message?   Yes / No

Guest Name: _____ Date Stayed: _____

Traveling From: _____ Weather: ☼ ☁ ☂ ❄ 🌡 🌡 ⚑ ☁

Favorite Memory / Recommended Activity:

_____

_____

_____

_____

Message:

_____

_____

_____

_____

_____

_____

May we share your message?   Yes / No

Guest Name: _____   Date Stayed: _____

Traveling From: _____   Weather: ☀ ⛅ ☔ ❄ 🌡 🌡 🚩 ☁

Favorite Memory / Recommended Activity:

_____

_____

_____

_____

Message:

_____

_____

_____

_____

_____

_____

May we share your message?   Yes / No

Guest Name: _____ Date Stayed: _____

Traveling From: _____ Weather: ☀ ☁ ☂ ❄ 🌡 🌡 🚩 ☁

Favorite Memory / Recommended Activity:

_____

_____

_____

_____

_____

Message:

_____

_____

_____

_____

_____

_____

_____

May we share your message?   Yes / No

Guest Name: _____ Date Stayed: _____

Traveling From: _____ Weather: ☀ ☁ ☂ ❄ 🌡 🌡 🚩 ☁

Favorite Memory / Recommended Activity:

_____

_____

_____

_____

_____

Message:

_____

_____

_____

_____

_____

_____

May we share your message?   Yes / No

Guest Name: _____   Date Stayed: _____

Traveling From: _____   Weather: ☀ ⛅ ☔ ❄ 🌡 🌡 🚩 ☁

Favorite Memory / Recommended Activity:

_____

_____

_____

_____

Message:

_____

_____

_____

_____

_____

May we share your message?   Yes / No

Guest Name: _____   Date Stayed: _____

Traveling From: _____   Weather: ☼ ☁ ☂ ❄ 🌡 🌡 🚩 ☁

Favorite Memory / Recommended Activity:

_____

_____

_____

_____

Message:

_____

_____

_____

_____

_____

_____

_____

May we share your message?   Yes / No

Guest Name: _____   Date Stayed: _____

Traveling From: _____   Weather: ☀ ⛅ ☂ ❄ 🌡 🌡 🚩 ☁

Favorite Memory / Recommended Activity:

_____

_____

_____

_____

_____

Message:

_____

_____

_____

_____

_____

_____

May we share your message?   Yes / No

Guest Name: _____ Date Stayed: _____

Traveling From: _____ Weather: ☀ ☁ ☂ ❄ 🌡 🌡 🚩 ☁

Favorite Memory / Recommended Activity:

_____

_____

_____

_____

_____

Message:

_____

_____

_____

_____

_____

_____

May we share your message?   Yes / No

Guest Name: _____ Date Stayed: _____

Traveling From: _____ Weather: ☀ ⛅ ☔ ❄ 🌡 🌡 🚩 ☁

Favorite Memory / Recommended Activity:

_____

_____

_____

_____

Message:

_____

_____

_____

_____

_____

_____

May we share your message?   Yes / No

Guest Name: _____ Date Stayed: _____

Traveling From: _____ Weather: ☀ ☁ ☔ ❄ 🌡 🌡 🚩 ☁

Favorite Memory / Recommended Activity:

_____

_____

_____

_____

Message:

_____

_____

_____

_____

_____

_____

May we share your message?   Yes / No

Guest Name: _____ Date Stayed: _____

Traveling From: _____ Weather: ☀ ⛅ ☔ ❄ 🌡 🌡 🚩 ☁

Favorite Memory / Recommended Activity:

_____

_____

_____

_____

Message:

_____

_____

_____

_____

_____

May we share your message?   Yes / No

Guest Name: _____   Date Stayed: _____

Traveling From: _____   Weather: ☀ ☁ ☂ ❄ 🌡 🌡 🚩 ☁

Favorite Memory / Recommended Activity:

_____

_____

_____

_____

_____

Message:

_____

_____

_____

_____

_____

_____

May we share your message?   Yes / No

Guest Name: _____   Date Stayed: _____

Traveling From: _____   Weather: ☀ ☁ ☂ ❄ 🌡 🌡 🚩 ☁

Favorite Memory / Recommended Activity:

_____

_____

_____

_____

Message:

_____

_____

_____

_____

_____

_____

May we share your message?   Yes / No

Guest Name: _____ Date Stayed: _____

Traveling From: _____ Weather: ☀ ⛅ ☂ ❄ 🌡 🌡 🏴 🍦

Favorite Memory / Recommended Activity:

_____

_____

_____

_____

Message:

_____

_____

_____

_____

_____

_____

May we share your message?   Yes / No

Guest Name: _____ Date Stayed: _____

Traveling From: _____ Weather: ☀ ☁ ☂ ❄ 🌡 🌡 🚩 ☂

Favorite Memory / Recommended Activity:

_____

_____

_____

_____

_____

Message:

_____

_____

_____

_____

_____

_____

_____

May we share your message?   Yes / No

Guest Name: _____ Date Stayed: _____

Traveling From: _____ Weather: ☼ ☁ ☂ ❄ 🌡 🌡 🚩 ☁

Favorite Memory / Recommended Activity:

_____

_____

_____

_____

Message:

_____

_____

_____

_____

_____

May we share your message?   Yes / No

Guest Name: _____   Date Stayed: _____

Traveling From: _____   Weather: ☀ ⛅ ☂ ❄ 🌡 🌡 🚩 ☁

Favorite Memory / Recommended Activity:

_____

_____

_____

_____

Message:

_____

_____

_____

_____

_____

_____

May we share your message?   Yes / No

Guest Name: _____ Date Stayed: _____

Traveling From: _____ Weather: ☀ ☁ ☂ ❄ 🌡 🌡 🚩 ☁

Favorite Memory / Recommended Activity:

_____

_____

_____

_____

_____

Message:

_____

_____

_____

_____

_____

_____

_____

May we share your message?   Yes / No

Guest Name: _____ Date Stayed: _____

Traveling From: _____ Weather: ☀ ⛅ ☔ ❄ 🌡 🌡 🚩 🍦

Favorite Memory / Recommended Activity:

_____

_____

_____

_____

Message:

_____

_____

_____

_____

_____

_____

May we share your message?   Yes / No

Guest Name: _____ Date Stayed: _____

Traveling From: _____ Weather: ☀ ☁ ☂ ❄ 🌡 🌡 🚩 🍦

Favorite Memory / Recommended Activity:

_____

_____

_____

_____

Message:

_____

_____

_____

_____

_____

_____

_____

May we share your message?   Yes / No

Guest Name: _____ Date Stayed: _____

Traveling From: _____ Weather: ☀ ⛅ ☔ ❄ 🌡 🌡 🚩 🌀

Favorite Memory / Recommended Activity:

_____

_____

_____

_____

Message:

_____

_____

_____

_____

_____

_____

May we share your message?   Yes / No

Guest Name: _____   Date Stayed: _____

Traveling From: _____   Weather: ☀ ☁ ☂ ❄ 🌡 🌡 🚩 ☁

Favorite Memory / Recommended Activity:

_____

_____

_____

_____

_____

Message:

_____

_____

_____

_____

_____

_____

_____

May we share your message?   Yes / No

Guest Name: _____ Date Stayed: _____

Traveling From: _____ Weather: ☼ ☁ ☂ ❄ 🌡 🌡 🚩 ☁

Favorite Memory / Recommended Activity:

_____

_____

_____

_____

_____

Message:

_____

_____

_____

_____

_____

_____

May we share your message?   Yes / No

Guest Name: _____ Date Stayed: _____

Traveling From: _____ Weather: ☀ ☁ ☂ ❄ 🌡 🌡 🚩 ☁

Favorite Memory / Recommended Activity:

_____

_____

_____

_____

_____

Message:

_____

_____

_____

_____

_____

_____

May we share your message?   Yes / No

Guest Name: _____   Date Stayed: _____

Traveling From: _____   Weather: ☀ ⛅ ☔ ❄ 🌡 🌡 🚩 ☁

Favorite Memory / Recommended Activity:

_____

_____

_____

_____

Message:

_____

_____

_____

_____

_____

May we share your message?   Yes / No

Guest Name: _____ Date Stayed: _____

Traveling From: _____ Weather: ☀ ☁ ☂ ❄ 🌡 🌡 🚩 ☁

Favorite Memory / Recommended Activity:

_____

_____

_____

_____

_____

Message:

_____

_____

_____

_____

_____

_____

May we share your message?   Yes / No

Guest Name: _____ Date Stayed: _____

Traveling From: _____ Weather: ☀ ☁ ☔ ❄ 🌡 🌡 🚩 ☁

Favorite Memory / Recommended Activity:

_____

_____

_____

_____

Message:

_____

_____

_____

_____

_____

_____

May we share your message?   Yes / No

Guest Name: _____ Date Stayed: _____

Traveling From: _____ Weather: ☀ ⛅ ☂ ❄ 🌡 🌡 🚩 ☁

Favorite Memory / Recommended Activity:

_____

_____

_____

_____

_____

Message:

_____

_____

_____

_____

_____

_____

May we share your message?   Yes / No

Guest Name: _____ Date Stayed: _____

Traveling From: _____ Weather: ☀ ⛅ ☔ ❄ 🌡 🌡 🚩 ☁

Favorite Memory / Recommended Activity:

_____

_____

_____

_____

Message:

_____

_____

_____

_____

_____

May we share your message?   Yes / No

Guest Name: _____	Date Stayed: _____

Traveling From: _____	Weather: ☀ ☁ ☂ ❄ 🌡 🌡 🏳 ☁

Favorite Memory / Recommended Activity:

_____

_____

_____

_____

_____

Message:

_____

_____

_____

_____

_____

_____

_____

May we share your message?   Yes / No

Guest Name: _____ Date Stayed: _____

Traveling From: _____ Weather: ☀ ⛅ ☔ ❄ 🌡 🌡 🚩 ☁

Favorite Memory / Recommended Activity:

_____

_____

_____

_____

_____

Message:

_____

_____

_____

_____

_____

May we share your message?   Yes / No

Guest Name: _____ Date Stayed: _____

Traveling From: _____ Weather: ☀ ☁ ☔ ❄ 🌡 🌡 🚩 ☁

Favorite Memory / Recommended Activity:

_____

_____

_____

_____

Message:

_____

_____

_____

_____

_____

May we share your message?   Yes / No

Guest Name: _____ Date Stayed: _____

Traveling From: _____ Weather: ☀ ⛅ ☔ ❄ 🌡 🌡 🏳 ☁

Favorite Memory / Recommended Activity:

_____

_____

_____

_____

Message:

_____

_____

_____

_____

_____

_____

May we share your message?   Yes / No

Guest Name: _____ Date Stayed: _____

Traveling From: _____ Weather: ☀ ⛅ ☔ ❄ 🌡 🌡 🚩 ☁

Favorite Memory / Recommended Activity:

_____

_____

_____

_____

Message:

_____

_____

_____

_____

_____

_____

May we share your message?   Yes / No

Guest Name: _____ Date Stayed: _____

Traveling From: _____ Weather: ☀ ⛅ ☔ ❄ 🌡 🌡 🚩 ☁

Favorite Memory / Recommended Activity:

_____

_____

_____

_____

Message:

_____

_____

_____

_____

_____

_____

May we share your message?   Yes / No

Guest Name: _____ Date Stayed: _____

Traveling From: _____ Weather: ☀ ☁ ☂ ❄ 🌡 🌡 🚩 ☁

Favorite Memory / Recommended Activity:

_____

_____

_____

_____

Message:

_____

_____

_____

_____

_____

_____

May we share your message?   Yes / No

Guest Name: _____ Date Stayed: _____

Traveling From: _____ Weather: ☀ ⛅ ☂ ❄ 🌡 🌡 🚩 ☁

Favorite Memory / Recommended Activity:

_____

_____

_____

_____

Message:

_____

_____

_____

_____

_____

_____

May we share your message?   Yes / No

Guest Name: _____ Date Stayed: _____

Traveling From: _____ Weather: ☀ ☁ ☂ ❄ 🌡 🌡 🏳 ☁

Favorite Memory / Recommended Activity:

_____

_____

_____

_____

_____

Message:

_____

_____

_____

_____

_____

_____

May we share your message?   Yes / No

Guest Name: _____ Date Stayed: _____

Traveling From: _____ Weather: ☀ ⛅ ☔ ❄ 🌡 🌡 🚩 ☁

Favorite Memory / Recommended Activity:

_____

_____

_____

_____

_____

Message:

_____

_____

_____

_____

_____

_____

May we share your message?   Yes / No

Guest Name: _____ Date Stayed: _____

Traveling From: _____ Weather: ☼ ☁ ☂ ❄ 🌡 🌡 🚩 🐚

Favorite Memory / Recommended Activity:

_____

_____

_____

_____

_____

Message:

_____

_____

_____

_____

_____

_____

May we share your message?   Yes / No

Guest Name: _____ Date Stayed: _____

Traveling From: _____ Weather: ☀ ⛅ ☔ ❄ 🌡 🌡 🚩 ☁

Favorite Memory / Recommended Activity:

_____

_____

_____

_____

Message:

_____

_____

_____

_____

_____

_____

May we share your message?   Yes / No

Guest Name: _____ Date Stayed: _____

Traveling From: _____ Weather: ☼ ☁ ☂ ❄ 🌡 🌡 🚩 ☁

Favorite Memory / Recommended Activity:

_____

_____

_____

_____

Message:

_____

_____

_____

_____

_____

_____

May we share your message?   Yes / No

Guest Name: _____ Date Stayed: _____

Traveling From: _____ Weather: ☀ ⛅ ☔ ❄ 🌡 🌡 🚩 ☁

Favorite Memory / Recommended Activity:

_____

_____

_____

_____

Message:

_____

_____

_____

_____

_____

_____

_____

May we share your message?   Yes / No

Guest Name: _____ Date Stayed: _____

Traveling From: _____ Weather: ☀ ⛅ ☂ ❄ 🌡 🌡 🚩 ☁

Favorite Memory / Recommended Activity:

_____

_____

_____

_____

_____

Message:

_____

_____

_____

_____

_____

_____

May we share your message?   Yes / No

Guest Name: _____ Date Stayed: _____

Traveling From: _____ Weather: ☀ ☁ ☔ ❄ 🌡 🌡 🚩 🌧

Favorite Memory / Recommended Activity:

_____

_____

_____

_____

Message:

_____

_____

_____

_____

_____

_____

May we share your message?   Yes / No

Guest Name: _____ Date Stayed: _____

Traveling From: _____ Weather: ☀ ☁ ☔ ❄ 🌡 🌡 🚩 ☁

Favorite Memory / Recommended Activity:

_____

_____

_____

_____

_____

Message:

_____

_____

_____

_____

_____

_____

May we share your message?   Yes / No

Guest Name: _____   Date Stayed: _____

Traveling From: _____   Weather: ☀ ⛅ ☔ ❄ 🌡 🌡 🚩 ☁

Favorite Memory / Recommended Activity:

_____

_____

_____

_____

Message:

_____

_____

_____

_____

_____

_____

May we share your message?   Yes / No

Guest Name: _____ Date Stayed: _____

Traveling From: _____ Weather: ☀ ☁ ☔ ❄ 🌡 🌡 🚩 ☁

Favorite Memory / Recommended Activity:

_____

_____

_____

_____

Message:

_____

_____

_____

_____

_____

_____

May we share your message?   Yes / No

Guest Name: _____   Date Stayed: _____

Traveling From: _____   Weather: ☼ ☁ ☂ ❄ 🌡 🌡 ⚑ ☁

Favorite Memory / Recommended Activity:

_____

_____

_____

_____

Message:

_____

_____

_____

_____

_____

_____

May we share your message?   Yes / No

Guest Name: _____ Date Stayed: _____

Traveling From: _____ Weather: ☀ ⛅ ☔ ❄ 🌡 🌡 🚩 ☁

Favorite Memory / Recommended Activity:

_____

_____

_____

_____

Message:

_____

_____

_____

_____

_____

_____

_____

May we share your message?   Yes / No

Guest Name: _____ Date Stayed: _____

Traveling From: _____ Weather: ☼ ☁ ☂ ❄ 🌡 🌡 🚩 ☁

Favorite Memory / Recommended Activity:

_____

_____

_____

_____

_____

Message:

_____

_____

_____

_____

_____

_____

_____

May we share your message?　　Yes　/　No

Guest Name: _____   Date Stayed: _____

Traveling From: _____   Weather: ☼ ☁ ☔ ❄ 🌡 🌡 🚩 🍦

Favorite Memory / Recommended Activity:

_____

_____

_____

_____

_____

Message:

_____

_____

_____

_____

_____

_____

May we share your message?   Yes / No

Guest Name: _____ Date Stayed: _____

Traveling From: _____ Weather: ☀ ⛅ ☂ ❄ 🌡 🌡 🚩 💨

Favorite Memory / Recommended Activity:

_____

_____

_____

_____

Message:

_____

_____

_____

_____

_____

_____

May we share your message?   Yes / No

Guest Name: _____ Date Stayed: _____

Traveling From: _____ Weather: ☀ ☁ ☂ ❄ 🌡 🌡 🚩 ☘

Favorite Memory / Recommended Activity:

_____

_____

_____

_____

_____

Message:

_____

_____

_____

_____

_____

_____

_____

May we share your message?　　Yes / No

Guest Name: _____ Date Stayed: _____

Traveling From: _____ Weather: ☀ ⛅ ☂ ❄ 🌡 🌡 🚩 ☁

Favorite Memory / Recommended Activity:

_____

_____

_____

_____

_____

Message:

_____

_____

_____

_____

_____

_____

_____

May we share your message?   Yes / No

Guest Name: _____ Date Stayed: _____

Traveling From: _____ Weather: ☀ ☁ ☔ ❄ 🌡 🌡 🚩 ⛅

Favorite Memory / Recommended Activity:

_____

_____

_____

_____

Message:

_____

_____

_____

_____

_____

_____

May we share your message?   Yes / No

Guest Name: _____ Date Stayed: _____

Traveling From: _____ Weather: ☀ ⛅ ☔ ❄ 🌡 🌡 🚩 💨

Favorite Memory / Recommended Activity:

_____

_____

_____

_____

Message:

_____

_____

_____

_____

_____

_____

May we share your message?   Yes / No

Guest Name: _____ Date Stayed: _____

Traveling From: _____ Weather: ☀ ⛅ ☔ ❄ 🌡 🌡 🚩 ☁

Favorite Memory / Recommended Activity:

_____

_____

_____

_____

Message:

_____

_____

_____

_____

_____

_____

_____

May we share your message?   Yes / No

Guest Name: _____   Date Stayed: _____

Traveling From: _____   Weather: ☀ ⛅ ☔ ❄ 🌡 🌡 🚩 ☁

Favorite Memory / Recommended Activity:

_____

_____

_____

_____

_____

Message:

_____

_____

_____

_____

_____

_____

_____

May we share your message?   Yes / No

Guest Name: _____ Date Stayed: _____

Traveling From: _____ Weather: ☀ ☁ ☂ ❄ 🌡 🌡 🚩 ☁

Favorite Memory / Recommended Activity:

_____

_____

_____

_____

Message:

_____

_____

_____

_____

_____

_____

_____

May we share your message?   Yes / No

Guest Name: _____   Date Stayed: _____

Traveling From: _____   Weather: ☀ ⛅ ☔ ❄ 🌡 🌡 🏴 ☁

Favorite Memory / Recommended Activity:

_____

_____

_____

_____

Message:

_____

_____

_____

_____

_____

_____

May we share your message?   Yes / No

Guest Name: _____ Date Stayed: _____

Traveling From: _____ Weather: ☀ ☁ ☂ ❄ 🌡 🌡 🚩 🌦

Favorite Memory / Recommended Activity:

_____

_____

_____

_____

Message:

_____

_____

_____

_____

_____

_____

May we share your message?   Yes / No

Guest Name: _____   Date Stayed: _____

Traveling From: _____   Weather: ☀ ☁ ☂ ❄ 🌡 🌡 ⚑ ☁

Favorite Memory / Recommended Activity:

_____

_____

_____

_____

Message:

_____

_____

_____

_____

_____

_____

May we share your message?   Yes / No

Guest Name: _____ Date Stayed: _____

Traveling From: _____ Weather: ☀ ☁ ☂ ❄ 🌡 🌡 🚩 ☁

Favorite Memory / Recommended Activity:

_____

_____

_____

_____

_____

Message:

_____

_____

_____

_____

_____

_____

May we share your message?   Yes / No

Guest Name: _____   Date Stayed: _____

Traveling From: _____   Weather: ☼ ☁ ☔ ❄ 🌡 🌡 🚩 💨

Favorite Memory / Recommended Activity:

_____

_____

_____

_____

Message:

_____

_____

_____

_____

_____

_____

May we share your message?   Yes / No

Guest Name: _____   Date Stayed: _____

Traveling From: _____   Weather: ☀ ⛅ ☔ ❄ 🌡 🌡 🚩 ☁

Favorite Memory / Recommended Activity:

_____

_____

_____

_____

Message:

_____

_____

_____

_____

_____

_____

May we share your message?   Yes / No

Guest Name: _____ Date Stayed: _____

Traveling From: _____ Weather: ☀ ⛅ ☔ ❄ 🌡 🌡 🚩 ☁

Favorite Memory / Recommended Activity:

_____

_____

_____

_____

_____

Message:

_____

_____

_____

_____

_____

_____

May we share your message?   Yes / No

Guest Name: _____ Date Stayed: _____

Traveling From: _____ Weather: ☀ ☁ ☂ ❄ 🌡 🌡 🚩 🐚

Favorite Memory / Recommended Activity:

_____

_____

_____

_____

_____

Message:

_____

_____

_____

_____

_____

_____

_____

May we share your message?   Yes / No

Guest Name: _____ Date Stayed: _____

Traveling From: _____ Weather: ☀ ⛅ ☔ ❄ 🌡 🌡 🚩 💨

Favorite Memory / Recommended Activity:

_____

_____

_____

_____

Message:

_____

_____

_____

_____

_____

_____

May we share your message?   Yes / No

Guest Name: _____ Date Stayed: _____

Traveling From: _____ Weather: ☀ ☁ ☂ ❄ 🌡 🌡 🚩 ☁

Favorite Memory / Recommended Activity:

_____

_____

_____

_____

Message:

_____

_____

_____

_____

_____

_____

May we share your message?   Yes / No

Guest Name: _____ Date Stayed: _____

Traveling From: _____ Weather: ☀ ⛅ ☔ ❄ 🌡 🌡 🚩 ☁

Favorite Memory / Recommended Activity:

_____

_____

_____

_____

_____

Message:

_____

_____

_____

_____

_____

_____

May we share your message?   Yes / No

Guest Name: _____ Date Stayed: _____

Traveling From: _____ Weather: ☀ ⛅ ☂ ❄ 🌡 🌡 🚩 ☁

Favorite Memory / Recommended Activity:

_____

_____

_____

_____

Message:

_____

_____

_____

_____

_____

May we share your message?   Yes / No

Guest Name: _____   Date Stayed: _____

Traveling From: _____   Weather: ☀ ⛅ ☔ ❄ 🌡 🌡 🚩 ☁

Favorite Memory / Recommended Activity:

_____

_____

_____

_____

Message:

_____

_____

_____

_____

_____

May we share your message?   Yes / No

Guest Name: _____ Date Stayed: _____

Traveling From: _____ Weather: ☀ ⛅ ☔ ❄ 🌡 🌡 🚩 ☁

Favorite Memory / Recommended Activity:

_____

_____

_____

_____

Message:

_____

_____

_____

_____

_____

_____

_____

May we share your message?   Yes / No

Guest Name: _____ Date Stayed: _____

Traveling From: _____ Weather: ☀ ⛅ ☔ ❄ 🌡 🌡 🚩 ☁

Favorite Memory / Recommended Activity:

_____

_____

_____

_____

Message:

_____

_____

_____

_____

_____

_____

May we share your message?   Yes / No

Guest Name: _____   Date Stayed: _____

Traveling From: _____   Weather: ☀ ⛅ ☔ ❄ 🌡 🌡 🚩 ☁

Favorite Memory / Recommended Activity:

_____

_____

_____

_____

Message:

_____

_____

_____

_____

_____

_____

May we share your message?   Yes / No

Guest Name: _____   Date Stayed: _____

Traveling From: _____ Weather: ☀ ⛅ ☔ ❄ 🌡 🌡 🚩 ☁

Favorite Memory / Recommended Activity:

_____

_____

_____

_____

Message:

_____

_____

_____

_____

_____

_____

May we share your message?   Yes / No

Guest Name: _____   Date Stayed: _____

Traveling From: _____   Weather: ☼ ☁ ☂ ❄ 🌡 🌡 ⚑ ☂

Favorite Memory / Recommended Activity:

_____

_____

_____

_____

_____

Message:

_____

_____

_____

_____

_____

_____

_____

_____

May we share your message?   Yes / No

Guest Name: _____   Date Stayed: _____

Traveling From: _____   Weather: ☀ ☁ ☂ ❄ 🌡 🌡 🚩 ☔

Favorite Memory / Recommended Activity:

_____

_____

_____

_____

_____

Message:

_____

_____

_____

_____

_____

_____

May we share your message?   Yes / No

Guest Name: _____ Date Stayed: _____

Traveling From: _____ Weather: ☀ ⛅ ☂ ❄ 🌡 🌡 🚩 ☁

Favorite Memory / Recommended Activity:

_____

_____

_____

_____

Message:

_____

_____

_____

_____

_____

_____

May we share your message?   Yes / No

Guest Name: _____ Date Stayed: _____

Traveling From: _____ Weather: ☀ ⛅ ☂ ❄ 🌡 🌡 🚩 ☁

Favorite Memory / Recommended Activity:

_____

_____

_____

_____

Message:

_____

_____

_____

_____

_____

_____

May we share your message?   Yes / No

Guest Name: _____ Date Stayed: _____

Traveling From: _____ Weather: ☀ ☁ ☂ ❄ 🌡 🌡 ⚑ ☁

Favorite Memory / Recommended Activity:

_____

_____

_____

_____

Message:

_____

_____

_____

_____

_____

_____

May we share your message?   Yes / No

Guest Name: _____   Date Stayed: _____

Traveling From: _____   Weather: ☀ ☁ ☂ ❄ 🌡 🌡 🚩 ☁

Favorite Memory / Recommended Activity:

_____

_____

_____

_____

Message:

_____

_____

_____

_____

_____

_____

May we share your message?   Yes / No

Guest Name: _____ Date Stayed: _____

Traveling From: _____ Weather: ☀ ☁ ☂ ❄ 🌡 🌡 🚩 ☁

Favorite Memory / Recommended Activity:

_____

_____

_____

_____

_____

Message:

_____

_____

_____

_____

_____

_____

_____

May we share your message?   Yes / No

Guest Name: _____   Date Stayed: _____

Traveling From: _____   Weather: ☀ ⛅ ☔ ❄ 🌡 🌡 🚩 ☁

Favorite Memory / Recommended Activity:

_____

_____

_____

_____

Message:

_____

_____

_____

_____

_____

_____

May we share your message?   Yes / No

Guest Name: _____ Date Stayed: _____

Traveling From: _____ Weather: ☀ ⛅ ☔ ❄ 🌡 🌡 🚩 ☁

Favorite Memory / Recommended Activity:

_____

_____

_____

_____

Message:

_____

_____

_____

_____

_____

_____

_____

May we share your message?   Yes / No

Guest Name: _____ Date Stayed: _____

Traveling From: _____ Weather: ☀ ⛅ ☔ ❄ 🌡 🌡 🚩 ☁

Favorite Memory / Recommended Activity:

_____

_____

_____

_____

_____

Message:

_____

_____

_____

_____

_____

_____

_____

May we share your message?   Yes / No

Guest Name: _____ Date Stayed: _____

Traveling From: _____ Weather: ☀ ☁ ☂ ❄ 🌡 🌡 🚩 ☁

Favorite Memory / Recommended Activity:

_____

_____

_____

_____

Message:

_____

_____

_____

_____

_____

_____

May we share your message?   Yes / No

Guest Name: _____ Date Stayed: _____

Traveling From: _____ Weather: ☼ ⛅ ☔ ❄ 🌡 🌡 🚩 💨

Favorite Memory / Recommended Activity:

_____

_____

_____

_____

Message:

_____

_____

_____

_____

_____

_____

May we share your message?   Yes / No

Guest Name: _____ Date Stayed: _____

Traveling From: _____ Weather: ☀ ☁ ☂ ❄ 🌡 🌡 🚩 ☁

Favorite Memory / Recommended Activity:

_____

_____

_____

_____

_____

Message:

_____

_____

_____

_____

_____

_____

_____

May we share your message?   Yes / No

Guest Name: _____ Date Stayed: _____

Traveling From: _____ Weather: ☀ ⛅ ☂ ❄ 🌡 🌡 🚩 ☁

Favorite Memory / Recommended Activity:

_____

_____

_____

_____

Message:

_____

_____

_____

_____

_____

_____

May we share your message?   Yes / No

Guest Name: _____   Date Stayed: _____

Traveling From: _____   Weather: ☀ ☁ ☂ ❄ 🌡 🌡 🏳 ☁

Favorite Memory / Recommended Activity:

_____

_____

_____

_____

_____

Message:

_____

_____

_____

_____

_____

_____

May we share your message?   Yes / No

Guest Name: _____ Date Stayed: _____

Traveling From: _____ Weather: ☼ ⛅ ☂ ❄ 🌡 🌡 🚩 ☁

Favorite Memory / Recommended Activity:

_____

_____

_____

_____

Message:

_____

_____

_____

_____

_____

_____

May we share your message?   Yes / No

Guest Name: _____ Date Stayed: _____

Traveling From: _____ Weather: ☀ ☁ ☂ ❄ 🌡 🌡 🚩 ☁

Favorite Memory / Recommended Activity:

_____

_____

_____

_____

_____

Message:

_____

_____

_____

_____

_____

_____

_____

May we share your message?   Yes / No

Guest Name: _____ Date Stayed: _____

Traveling From: _____ Weather: ☀ ☁ ☔ ❄ 🌡 🌡 🚩 ☁

Favorite Memory / Recommended Activity:

_____

_____

_____

_____

Message:

_____

_____

_____

_____

_____

_____

May we share your message?   Yes / No

Guest Name: _____ Date Stayed: _____

Traveling From: _____ Weather: ☼ ☁ ☂ ❄ 🌡 🌡 🚩 ☁

Favorite Memory / Recommended Activity:

_____

_____

_____

_____

Message:

_____

_____

_____

_____

_____

_____

May we share your message?   Yes / No

Guest Name: _____ Date Stayed: _____

Traveling From: _____ Weather: ☀ ⛅ ☔ ❄ 🌡 🌡 🚩 🌳

Favorite Memory / Recommended Activity:

_____

_____

_____

_____

Message:

_____

_____

_____

_____

_____

May we share your message?   Yes / No

Guest Name: _____ Date Stayed: _____

Traveling From: _____ Weather: ☀ ⛅ ☂ ❄ 🌡 🌡 🚩 ☁

Favorite Memory / Recommended Activity:

_____

_____

_____

_____

_____

Message:

_____

_____

_____

_____

_____

_____

May we share your message?   Yes / No

Guest Name: _____ Date Stayed: _____

Traveling From: _____ Weather: ☀ ☁ ☂ ❄ 🌡 🌡 🚩 ☁

Favorite Memory / Recommended Activity:

_____

_____

_____

_____

Message:

_____

_____

_____

_____

_____

_____

May we share your message?   Yes / No

Guest Name: _____ Date Stayed: _____

Traveling From: _____ Weather: ☀ ☁ ☂ ❄ 🌡 🌡 🚩 🍦

Favorite Memory / Recommended Activity:

_____

_____

_____

_____

_____

Message:

_____

_____

_____

_____

_____

_____

_____

May we share your message?   Yes / No

Guest Name: _____ Date Stayed: _____

Traveling From: _____ Weather: ☀ ⛅ ☔ ❄ 🌡 🌡 🚩 ☁

Favorite Memory / Recommended Activity:

_____

_____

_____

_____

Message:

_____

_____

_____

_____

_____

_____

May we share your message?   Yes / No

Guest Name: _____ Date Stayed: _____

Traveling From: _____ Weather: ☀ ☁ ☂ ❄ 🌡 🌡 🚩 🌩

Favorite Memory / Recommended Activity:

_____

_____

_____

_____

Message:

_____

_____

_____

_____

_____

_____

May we share your message?   Yes / No

Guest Name: _____ Date Stayed: _____

Traveling From: _____ Weather: ☀ ⛅ ☔ ❄ 🌡 🌡 🚩 ☁

Favorite Memory / Recommended Activity:

_____

_____

_____

_____

_____

Message:

_____

_____

_____

_____

_____

_____

May we share your message?   Yes / No

Guest Name: _____ Date Stayed: _____

Traveling From: _____ Weather: ☀ ☁ ☔ ❄ 🌡 🌡 🚩 ☁

Favorite Memory / Recommended Activity:

_____

_____

_____

_____

_____

Message:

_____

_____

_____

_____

_____

_____

May we share your message?   Yes / No

Guest Name: _____ Date Stayed: _____

Traveling From: _____ Weather: ☀ ⛅ ☔ ❄ 🌡 🌡 🚩 ☁

Favorite Memory / Recommended Activity:

_____

_____

_____

_____

Message:

_____

_____

_____

_____

_____

_____

May we share your message?   Yes / No

Guest Name: _____ Date Stayed: _____

Traveling From: _____ Weather: ☀ ⛅ ☂ ❄ 🌡 🌡 🚩 ☁

Favorite Memory / Recommended Activity:

_____

_____

_____

_____

Message:

_____

_____

_____

_____

_____

_____

May we share your message?   Yes / No

Guest Name: _____ Date Stayed: _____

Traveling From: _____ Weather: ☀ ⛅ ☔ ❄ 🌡 🌡 🚩 ☁

Favorite Memory / Recommended Activity:

_____

_____

_____

_____

_____

Message:

_____

_____

_____

_____

_____

_____

May we share your message?   Yes / No

Guest Name: _____   Date Stayed: _____

Traveling From: _____   Weather: ☀ ☁ ☂ ❄ 🌡 🌡 🚩 🐚

Favorite Memory / Recommended Activity:

_____

_____

_____

_____

Message:

_____

_____

_____

_____

_____

_____

May we share your message?   Yes / No

Guest Name: _____ Date Stayed: _____

Traveling From: _____ Weather: ☀ ⛅ ☔ ❄ 🌡 🌡 🚩 ☁

Favorite Memory / Recommended Activity:

_____

_____

_____

_____

Message:

_____

_____

_____

_____

_____

_____

May we share your message?   Yes / No

Guest Name: _____ Date Stayed: _____

Traveling From: _____ Weather: ☀ ☁ ☂ ❄ 🌡 🌡 ⚑ ☁

Favorite Memory / Recommended Activity:

_____

_____

_____

_____

_____

Message:

_____

_____

_____

_____

_____

_____

_____

May we share your message?   Yes / No

Guest Name: _____ Date Stayed: _____

Traveling From: _____ Weather: ☀ ⛅ ☔ ❄ 🌡 🌡 🚩 ☁

Favorite Memory / Recommended Activity:

_____

_____

_____

_____

Message:

_____

_____

_____

_____

_____

May we share your message?   Yes / No

Guest Name: _____ Date Stayed: _____

Traveling From: _____ Weather: ☀ ☁ ☔ ❄ 🌡 🌡 🚩 ☁

Favorite Memory / Recommended Activity:

_____

_____

_____

_____

Message:

_____

_____

_____

_____

_____

_____

_____

May we share your message?   Yes / No

Guest Name: _____ Date Stayed: _____

Traveling From: _____ Weather: ☀ ⛅ ☂ ❄ 🌡 🌡 🚩 ☁

Favorite Memory / Recommended Activity:

_____

_____

_____

_____

Message:

_____

_____

_____

_____

_____

_____

May we share your message?   Yes / No

Guest Name: _____ Date Stayed: _____

Traveling From: _____ Weather: ☀ ☁ ☂ ❄ 🌡 🌡 🚩 ☁

Favorite Memory / Recommended Activity:

_____

_____

_____

_____

Message:

_____

_____

_____

_____

_____

_____

May we share your message?   Yes / No

Guest Name: _____ Date Stayed: _____

Traveling From: _____ Weather: ☀ ⛅ 🌂 ❄ 🌡 🌡 🚩 ☁

Favorite Memory / Recommended Activity:

_____

_____

_____

_____

Message:

_____

_____

_____

_____

_____

_____

May we share your message?   Yes / No

Guest Name: _____   Date Stayed: _____

Traveling From: _____   Weather: ☀ ☁ ☂ ❄ 🌡 🌡 🚩 ☁

Favorite Memory / Recommended Activity:

_____

_____

_____

_____

Message:

_____

_____

_____

_____

_____

_____

May we share your message?   Yes / No

Guest Name: _____ Date Stayed: _____

Traveling From: _____ Weather: ☀ ⛅ ☂ ❄ 🌡 🌡 🚩 ☁

Favorite Memory / Recommended Activity:

_____

_____

_____

_____

Message:

_____

_____

_____

_____

_____

_____

May we share your message?   Yes / No

Guest Name: _____ Date Stayed: _____

Traveling From: _____ Weather: ☀ ☁ ☂ ❄ 🌡 🌡 🚩 ☁

Favorite Memory / Recommended Activity:

_____

_____

_____

_____

Message:

_____

_____

_____

_____

_____

_____

May we share your message?   Yes / No

Guest Name: _____   Date Stayed: _____

Traveling From: _____   Weather: ☀ ⛅ ☔ ❄ 🌡 🌡 🚩 ☁

Favorite Memory / Recommended Activity:

_____

_____

_____

_____

Message:

_____

_____

_____

_____

_____

_____

May we share your message?   Yes / No

Guest Name: _____   Date Stayed: _____

Traveling From: _____   Weather: ☼ ☁ ☂ ❄ 🌡 🌡 🚩 ☁

Favorite Memory / Recommended Activity:

_____

_____

_____

_____

_____

Message:

_____

_____

_____

_____

_____

_____

May we share your message?   Yes / No

Guest Name: _____ Date Stayed: _____

Traveling From: _____ Weather: ☼ ☁ ☂ ❄ 🌡 🌡 🚩 ☁

Favorite Memory / Recommended Activity:

_____

_____

_____

_____

Message:

_____

_____

_____

_____

_____

_____

May we share your message?   Yes / No

Guest Name: _____   Date Stayed: _____

Traveling From: _____   Weather: ☀ ☁ ☂ ❄ 🌡 🌡 🚩 ☁

Favorite Memory / Recommended Activity:

_____

_____

_____

_____

_____

Message:

_____

_____

_____

_____

_____

_____

May we share your message?   Yes / No

Guest Name: _____ Date Stayed: _____

Traveling From: _____ Weather: ☀ ⛅ ☔ ❄ 🌡 🌡 🚩 ☁

Favorite Memory / Recommended Activity:

_____

_____

_____

_____

Message:

_____

_____

_____

_____

_____

May we share your message?　Yes　/　No

Guest Name: _____ Date Stayed: _____

Traveling From: _____ Weather: ☀ ☁ ☔ ❄ 🌡 🌡 🚩 ☁

Favorite Memory / Recommended Activity:

_____

_____

_____

_____

_____

Message:

_____

_____

_____

_____

_____

_____

May we share your message?   Yes / No

Guest Name: _____   Date Stayed: _____

Traveling From: _____   Weather: ☀ ⛅ ☂ ❄ 🌡 🌡 🚩 ☁

Favorite Memory / Recommended Activity:

_____

_____

_____

_____

Message:

_____

_____

_____

_____

_____

_____

May we share your message?   Yes / No

Guest Name: _____ Date Stayed: _____

Traveling From: _____ Weather: ☀ ☁ ☂ ❄ 🌡 🌡 🚩 ☁

Favorite Memory / Recommended Activity:

_____

_____

_____

_____

_____

Message:

_____

_____

_____

_____

_____

_____

May we share your message?   Yes / No

Guest Name: _____ Date Stayed: _____

Traveling From: _____ Weather: ☀ ⛅ ☂ ❄ 🌡 🌡 🚩 ☁

Favorite Memory / Recommended Activity:

_____

_____

_____

_____

_____

Message:

_____

_____

_____

_____

_____

_____

May we share your message?   Yes / No

Guest Name: _____ Date Stayed: _____

Traveling From: _____ Weather: ☀ ☁ ☂ ❄ 🌡 🌡 🚩 🍦

Favorite Memory / Recommended Activity:

_____

_____

_____

_____

_____

Message:

_____

_____

_____

_____

_____

_____

May we share your message?   Yes / No

Guest Name: _____   Date Stayed: _____

Traveling From: _____   Weather: ☀ ⛅ ☔ ❄ 🌡 🌡 🚩 ☁

Favorite Memory / Recommended Activity:

_____

_____

_____

_____

Message:

_____

_____

_____

_____

_____

_____

May we share your message?   Yes / No

Guest Name: _____   Date Stayed: _____

Traveling From: _____   Weather: ☀ ☁ ☂ ❄ 🌡 🌡 🚩 ☁

Favorite Memory / Recommended Activity:

_____

_____

_____

_____

_____

Message:

_____

_____

_____

_____

_____

_____

May we share your message?   Yes / No

Guest Name: _____   Date Stayed: _____

Traveling From: _____   Weather: ☀ ☁ ☂ ❄ 🌡 🌡 🚩 ☁

Favorite Memory / Recommended Activity:

_____

_____

_____

_____

_____

Message:

_____

_____

_____

_____

_____

_____

May we share your message?   Yes / No

Guest Name: _____ Date Stayed: _____

Traveling From: _____ Weather: ☀ ⛅ ☔ ❄ 🌡 🌡 🚩 ☁

Favorite Memory / Recommended Activity:

_____

_____

_____

_____

Message:

_____

_____

_____

_____

_____

May we share your message?   Yes / No

Guest Name: _____ Date Stayed: _____

Traveling From: _____ Weather: ☼ ☁ ☂ ❄ 🌡 🌡 🚩 ☁

Favorite Memory / Recommended Activity:

_____

_____

_____

_____

Message:

_____

_____

_____

_____

_____

_____

May we share your message?   Yes / No

Guest Name: _____ Date Stayed: _____

Traveling From: _____ Weather: ☀ ☁ ☂ ❄ 🌡 🌡 ⚑ ☁

Favorite Memory / Recommended Activity:

_____

_____

_____

_____

Message:

_____

_____

_____

_____

_____

_____

_____

May we share your message?   Yes / No

Made in the USA
Las Vegas, NV
26 August 2023

76647694R00083